LIFE PHILOSOPHIES AT 20

Essays on the fundamentals that encompass
the young person's life.

Martin Chomba

ISBN-13: 9798635999042

Cover design by: Martin Chomba
Library of Congress Control Number: 2018675309
Printed in the United States of America

FOREWORD

This book came as a result of the outpouring of ideas that haunt me to share them not just because of the content, but because of what it means for our generation.

For the people who read the draft and gave feedback that has helped shape the book to what it is now, am forever greatful.

INTRODUCTION

'Life philosophies at 20' is a collection of personal essays that explore my ideas with respect to various themes that encompass a 'millennial's' life. It attempts to debunk the myth that only the aged can claim wisdom and that young people can't have a voice that perpetuates philosophical ideas.

My aim is to talk about Africa in a different light by sparking a conversation that combines critical thought and experiences from the young mind's perspective. I am passionate about abstract fundamentals of life because of how important they are especially in a world where you can be anything you want.

LIFE PHILOSOPHIES AT 20

CONTENTS

♦ ♦ ♦

CHAPTER 1

Wisdom.

◆ ◆ ◆

Sam just couldn't see colour. He never bothered for it anyway.

Depression is Awesome! -or at least it is when you are not adding a noose or rat poison to your online shopping cart. It rips you up psychologically, physically, spiritually, perpendicularly, you name it. It's unapologetic, disdainful, desolation and desperation all in a cocktail that wreaks hopelessness. It strips you, gives you slaps on the face with no apology, and then gives you a sloppy kiss on the cheek that gives even Judas, in all his menacing glory, the chills.

I don't blame poor Sam, his story is akin to many that fuel the 'self-help economy' as I like to call it; booming with self-acclaimed life-coaches, mentors, and self-help authors. He was top of his job working on the wall street of Nairobi city: Upperhill, chatting up business men and women with his undeniable charm. I can pretend to know what his exact job was, but in all honesty, I have no idea what they really do up there. I imagine suits, relentless beeping of phones, and papers all written in heavy business jargon strewn in every corner; a hill of controlled chaos that controls the economy through literal scribbles on the bottom of pages. Sam was all that and a bag of chips; he wore the dry-cleaned suits, managed a team of financers, and managed to do all that while carrying a water bottle with 2 or 3 decolourised lemon slices. His life seemed normal to say the least, but deep down, he was rotting; building up to his crescendo of a breakdown. Nothing was going right, things at home were thick and his job was draining his very soul. Unfulfilled and unhappy, he raised the white flag to the crumbling cookie. The fat lady had finally sang; he had had enough. What followed was a series of books highlighting what he christened his re-awakening. He was transformed; now a life coach and motivational speaker, he shared his 'moment of epiphany' and highlighted his principles of life through his life story in a bid to inspire and change the world in his own small way.

Depression is a state of emergency. What I call a normal reaction to a crisis in desperate need of audit. Reality has just given you an 'F' in life and now all the unfiltered trash that your mind had taken to cognition all these years has now piled up to create a state of cognitive dissonance that needs to be resolved now! All the ideas from quotes, beliefs, sermons, books and seminars you have read and heard, are all null now. The rudiments of your very existence have to be re-built from scratch. Sam's story is a textbook representation of this process. It is through this kind of overhaul that we gain wisdom and define our ideal life.

When I was younger, I imagined that it was only through age and experience that one could be christened with the coveted title of being a wise man or woman. What I've come to be aware of now is that we can re-live the experiences of others through any form of mental stimulation and interpret them for wisdom because what really matters is the lessons drawn from said experiences rather than how long it takes us. It could be through an oral story, a documentary, or a book, but either way, one that highlights a real experience that's re-livable. The whole idea of wisdom is based on experiences; think of it as the ten-thousand-hours rule but now with experiences; therefore, the premise of age insurmountably being intertwined to wisdom is a dogmatic approach we ought to abandon, all age does is give an extra edge time-wise that allows more experiences and thus more lessons, the time we spend experiencing and deriving these lessons is what we sum up as age and we perceive it as being proportional to wisdom which is ideally not fallacious but a rather grammatical confinement that makes the innate idea of experience and lessons; the holy grail of wisdom, a behind the scenes concept.

Wisdom for me reads as a knowing that equips you for any given situation; it's a mastery of life that can't be exhaustively documented. It's not knowledge of all scientific concepts or all the ways to act like a gentleman; it is the relationship between all that and life. A wise person combines new knowledge with pre-existing knowledge to predict the future and evaluate possible outcomes of action. Wise men and women –not astrologers or fortune tellers- are just like you and me who appreciate and have preserved the role that critical thought plays in determining the causes of actions.

A young man named 'Kamau' was engaged in a team building exercise. Among the activities lined up to this effect, was a simple exercise where the larger group was divided into smaller ones to come up with names and a slogan. Kamau approached his group with a mentality that did not in any way presuppose that his group had to win; but rather, he understood that the greater objective at hand was to have fun and bond. Another young man in the same group wasn't as open-minded and that was evident in the fact that he really tried to impose his ideas on the group in a text book display of insufficient emotional intelligence. Our open-minded team player on the other hand, understood clearly that the idea of a perfect group to him did not exist. He understood that accommodating so many people meant not only making personal compromises, but also accommodating his antagonist; so to speak. Our young man took every opportunity presented to him to listen to everyone's opinion as presented and

critic with restraint, fully cognizant of the fact that the import-
ance of a simple activity such as finding a group name did not lie
in the name itself, but rather the experience. Running with that
same train of thought, all ideas would have been good, and pref-
erence should have been on the catchiest of names that leave a
lasting impression on the rival groups as well as intimidate them.
So basically, it was a matter of consensus rather than the illusion
of a prefect name. The group ended up picking Kamau as their
leader since the general population felt more comfortable under
his command.

It's a simple analogy that juxtaposes two individuals thinking in the short-term and long-term. One who thinks in the long
term shows wisdom in his thought since he considers more factors before coming to a conclusion.

I think of being rendered smart as clever thinking in the
short term and wisdom as thinking in the long term. It is safe to
infer that everyone of sound mind engages in philosophical
thought at some point in their lives, and it leaves them enlight-
ened on their life destiny. We live by how we think; it is through
philosophizing that we acquire the fundamentals of what living
to us means. We identify an instance that requires critical mental
input to provide the most sober judgment; which goes without
mentioning, is determined by our past experiences. We ponder
on said predicament, analyzing the intricacies and trees of
thought to determine the right course of action. It is the conclusion to this train of thought that shapes our thinking and in general; our life philosophy. Like Sam, this moment can be triggered
by a life event that forces us to go back to the drawing board. The
idea of how strongly we hold on to our beliefs in what's defined as
our level of open-mindedness is more a subjective drawing than
an objective one. The rigid hold their beliefs so closely that it is
hard to change their mind once set, even with the clear identifica-
tion of errors in their reasoning; they still hold on to said beliefs
not because they do not see their fault, but because that is the

whole framework of their reality that has been shaped in one way or another by their values, culture, religion etc. The open-minded live their lives knowing that their beliefs could change any moment. They live by one belief at an instance but are ready to listen to any that are contrary and critically rip it out limb by limb to see how well it holds up against the objective at hand in a non-hostile approach not littered with thoughts of immediate ridicule or condemnation at face value, but rather equal treatment of ideas, and it is how well it argues itself out that determines whether it could suffice. The latter is what I live by and it is in my view, the best way of living in today's world: It expresses that one isn't capable of knowing everything with absolute certainty but rather, life is a continuum of knowledge that has different phases of determining how one can truly claim to know. It is also an expression of how one man is not sufficient by himself, but rather depends on his fellow beings to acquire knowledge and to analyze it. An open-mind is thirsty for knowledge and isn't afraid to state that it was wrong when categorically disproved. It constantly questions its beliefs and re-evaluates them day in day out based on newly acquired knowledge and the greatest gift of all; introspection. We are constantly evolving as human beings thanks to new discoveries every day, and a wise man has to be one always on his toes for knowledge that spans far, wide and deep.

When I was started out on the bass guitar, I used to have a hard time understanding why I was learning some things. I questioned all the dexterity exercises and argued them out with my teacher since I knew the playing that would be demanded of me was inclined towards a much more limited scope of genres than I was practicing for, so it just didn't make sense spending so much time learning something I would never use —kind of like our perception on specific ideas taught in our education system— or so I thought. Ultimately, after grueling hours of exercises at painful speeds of 30bpm, (you'd think playing faster is what's harder) I could see it reflect in my playing. I was more versatile and I could put a lick or a really fast run here and there that I never imagined

I could. As time went by, it was demanded of me to be more versatile and play beyond what I had set out to play, and all the once meaningless exercises made the transition as smooth as I would have wanted. It's not about where you think you might apply it but it's a matter of having it to apply and that's the intricate aspect of knowledge I haven't quite gotten a grasp on because it disproves all our envisioned goals by telling us it is in charge and we have to trust it with more of our hearts than our brains that we will achieve greatness. There is so much information out there that we don't even know where to begin, and when we finally set our mind on one, life throws us another curve-ball.

What I revel in most when it comes to knowledge is how ideas and concepts when broken down to their substance aren't new, but rather, it is their unique combinations that make them stand out. Gravity has always existed, all Isaac Newton did was simply point it out and put it to words, and better yet, on paper. Uber, a multibillion dollar company took transport; an age old concept in the name of taxis and combined it with technology. It seems to me that this way of thinking rewards us, so it's heartening to know that however abstract or far-fetched an idea or concept of knowledge is from our vision; it plays some role in our greatness I can't put on paper. So In case you wanted to become a professional classical pianist at some point and wondered what how many moles are in a litre of sulphuric acid have to do with any of that, my answer is: exactly! A wise person combines new knowledge with pre-existing knowledge to predict the future and evaluate the possible outcomes of actions. Wise men and women not astrologers or fortune tellers- are just like you and me who appreciate and have preserved the role that critical thought plays in determining causes of actions.

Books are great! I love books; In fact, I loved them so much I wrote one myself. I've learned the hard way that for some, it is better to just flip through pictures of turds than read them (just be sure not to lick your fingers). It was in my high school days that I encountered some terrible subject books that you could tell right off the cover were aimed at pure profit. Yeah, yeah…don't judge a book by its cover, tell it to the judge! I mean, how can so many answers be wrong!? It's a question and answer book for Christ sake! But I digress. Books are still great but none is omniscient and though that may stem from a point of subconscious trauma cum skepticism, I still view every book under a high magnification microscope. Sure, there may be an 'Ahaa!' moment where a book just speaks directly to your soul and you agree so vigorously with it that it automatically becomes your life manual, but be careful; no one man or woman on earth has the full-proof formula or so to speak 'holy grail' for how human beings should live their lives. Heck! We don't even know definitively why we are here in the first place, everyone seems to have an idea so who's right? I envy the Israelites because they seemed to have had their work cut out, their sole purpose was to get to the 'Promised land', it's all they had to do when they woke up, forget morning routines and makeup tutorials, when you were born, all you needed to know is who's in charge and how to walk like a wanderer. Today, a new self-help book with a glossy cover christened 'seven ways to be happy' just next to what seems to be the man with the most un-believable smile ever –kudos to the graphic designer by the way– comes out as the bestseller and we adore the authors with their all so glorious 'yoda' wisdom. I know this is hypocritical but I'd probably be among the first to grab a copy though I approach them with skepticism.

All ideas are in writing, I just haven't read enough to prove it. What every new book is doing is combining them differently and using words Shakespeare didn't. All those men and women had and have minds just like you, sure, you may consider them more intelligent, but when you think about it critically, their ideas are at your disposal and you now have the privilege of two minds: yours and the author's. When you read more, a whole lot more minds and ultimately, a crowd of scientists; ordinary men and women and scholars sited in a committee that helps you with every single decision you make. You can outrightly critique their thoughts based on your own life evaluations and other experiences you have lived through in the eyes of others, just don't put too much trust in others and you'll be okay.

We all have those intrinsic characteristics in our lives that drive us and that determine what we carve out on the stone that's earth. We just have to combine what life throws at us with the uniqueness we have: from our genetic fingerprint, to our childhood, which drawing from one of the greatest psychologist of ancient times is the period that largely shapes our lives, from how many times you were told a bedtime story as a child, to the kind of positive or negative reinforcement you received for doing good or bad, and even to those childhood experiences that we all dread in the name of daddy issues.

I know for a fact that everyone has some wisdom to share; some may be deeper than others, but regardless of age, we can all pick up the mic and express our thoughts on an issue based on premises derived from relevant experiences. I am here to have a conversation with the most people I can reach with the hope that it sparks philosophical thought with the aim of improving on existing ideologies. I don't believe wisdom can be taught because wisdom in itself should not be rigid in terms of thought, but rather, everyone should be entitled to their own independent principles, and it is how well said principles are argued out juxtaposed to the issue at hand and pre-existing ideologies that should really matter. It should be a battle of the minds where the best argument suffices for the moment as it awaits dethroning by a far more conclusive and holistic proposition. We should aim at constantly having the ball rolling when it comes to arguing out philosophical ideas. When many people come together and present their arguments and ideas on a common issue, then, factors others did not consider while formulating their arguments will arise. As the conversation proceeds, they will identify each other's faults and come up with a stronger argument that considers a wider array of premises with minimal fallacies and errors. This is in a nutshell, is the aim of the ideas I share here, though one-sided, it gives me the least bit of satisfaction knowing that I am giving the ball a nudge. We all have our theories on the ultimate way of living, we may or may not consider it the ultimate way, but they are all worth disrupting air molecules and I encourage you to spread all those ideas however you can but obviously within reason. Just like in Sam's case, there are conundrums and frustrations that make us feel as if we can't really make headway in our lives, but it is by sharing our own experiences and lessons that we save others the stress and time wasted trying to ruffle through difficult times looking for their lesson.

Let's look at an idea that has revolutionized my outlook on life. Every action has layers, and the more we peel, the more we reveal. We can peel further back from what we consider the immediate desire our actions are trying to fulfill, to the fundamental need that forms the core around which that desire is layered; think of it as the vision and mission of your life. Let's take a church for example. There is so much going on: from music to prayer groups to retreats, missions and so much more that it is easy to lose track of why you are really there. The church is built on the foundation of being a place of worship that entrenches God's word. You might be there because of a girl on the worship team whose legs look more heavenly than heaven itself or 'handsome Hillary' with his rugged beard that makes Idris Alba look like the rejected clone, or the worship team that has two Ariana Grande's and a Beyonce to spare, they might be the reason(s) you are there and might have actually kept you all this while, but that's not the core. Even if that lady had miniature legs on her actual legs, or the resident Idris took a leave of absence from the pool of singles, or even the worship team seems to have out of the blues, completely discarded the concept of a common key and why it's important, the church should be able to survive without all those things because that's not what the church is built on, it's built on the word and the true value of belief in God, and when we peel even further we find out that people come there to make an investment in the after-life. Another peel and we see the desire to be happy; not legs, not 'Hillary'; not music, not the word; not heaven but eternal happiness.

Think of this like a pyramid that shows you how your desires are structured. An interesting example we can't ignore, especially after using the word pyramid, is the hierarchy of human needs coined by Abraham Maslow. The basic need to find shelter and food and all that other yada yada we need is ultimately geared towards self-actualization, so what if we could achieve that same self-actualization in a different way? What if we don't have to go to school, get a job, get capital, start a business, become rich, and then finally become happy? What if we just jumped all the hurdles, peeled back all the layers and went for the larger desire that's at the apex of all that? This is an approach that moves desires from the specific to the general to open up opportunities for all the ways of achieving the general goal.

At the apex of most actions or even all, is the desire to be happy. There are so many things that can make one happy so we need to find a route that for the most part has already been conditioned in our brains by the way we were brought up. We can't for example; take drugs even though they will make us feel super happy because they contravene our moral code and that in itself would make us unhappy through guilt. We have also been pre-conditioned to having our happiness tied to that of the people around us: we are happy when they are happy and they are happy when we are happy so all that bloatware needs to be considered since ideally, happiness is just a bunch of chemicals in the brain. Interestingly, we have also been pre-conditioned to believe that no one thing can give us satisfactory happiness for the rest of our lives. Even for heaven, I at times wonder what will really be going on for all that period; I mean, will we be singing all day in a monotone all-white place just walking around in heavenly glory and bliss? That sounds tiring from an earthly perspective. We have also been pre-conditioned to wanting things, things that ought to bring us this happiness we seek: a new car, a better paying job, winning the lottery, a trophy wife, a big house, jewelry, the list is endless. From Mark Manson's counterintuitive perspective in 'The Subtle Art of Not giving a f*ck', we have also been preconditioned to expecting happiness after adversary so we simply plunge ourselves in said adversary to reach the pot of gold at the end of the rainbow. Going by all this, happiness is complicated and what complicates it even more is the time factor. To use this approach effectively we need to master how to peel back the layers from happiness and establish the most appropriate pattern of behavior that will lead us there faster. It's a chess game but now with real life and a million pieces to be moved.

Fiona has been working at a restaurant for two years now and is trying to save up for the dream she has wanted since she was a young kid. Her goal is to own her own restaurant and she already has a plan in place. She sets aside cash from her regular salary as part of savings for culinary school. She plans to becomes a chef at a popular restaurant and after rising through the ranks and becoming head chef, quit and use the money she's saved up to open her own restaurant. The layers here are: money then school, then a chef, then more money, then her own restaurant and ultimately happiness. If we peel back those layers, we see that before happiness, what she really wants is to fulfill her childhood dream of owning a restaurant that will ultimately lead to happiness. How can she get there faster? What if she quits her job all together and focuses on looking for money for school instead? What if she looked for a scholarship, or applied for student loans, or really, anything that will get her to school faster? What if instead of waiting until she has enough experience, she decided to bring together a team of other chefs with the same vision and pool resources together to simply start instead of aiming for perfection? These are all possibilities. Am not really teaching a new concept here, am just stating the obvious, we do it all the time, probably sub-consciously and it sounds so trivial but it's really our open-mindedness that lets us pursue these branches of possibilities and being conscious about it stacks up a whole lot more odds in your favour. Again, life is a game of chess with a million pieces to be moved, it's all about the fastest to checkmate. Try and picture the larger objective by peeling back the layers then start from there.

CHAPTER 2

Touched As a Child.

◆ ◆ ◆

Africa is a backward country; a shit-hole where genocide, perpetual war, dictatorship, ridiculous inflation, and apartheid, just to mention a few, provide statistics of what countries ought not to do. We are hungry and we live like monkeys. "Children dying in Africa from hunger" is a Hollywood catchphrase ditto to how we overwhelm the insatiable need for charitable organization to have a cause. We are the heart of Ebola. We have resources we seem not to not value and subsequently protect.

You see, the thing about home is that it will always be that, a home; a haven that you can't deny even by denying. It baptizes you with responsibility you never asked for the moment you breathe it's air regardless of whether it's keeping the house clean, watering the flowers or even making corruption a tad bit less of a nuisance, it gives you a purpose, and what's there not to love about having a purpose to fix what's wrong. It's all true, a hard truth that we have to grapple with, but one we need not take to heart but to action. I have come to believe that every problem has fruits, leaves, branches, a stem, and roots. To adequately evaluate the fruits that are our present problems, I want us to go back in time to identify the root of our issues; Africa was touched as a child, welcome to therapy.

Our chapter is set in the pre-dominantly lush greenery of Sub-Saharan Africa, where the discoverers arrived and found the people of Africa: dark, naked and basking in their all primordial glory. A place riddled with illiteracy and no sign or western civilization. It was a time when Africans never documented anything; knowledge was passed down orally in form of stories that inevitably became distorted somewhere along the way or died altogether when a catastrophic plague or war struck. Families were large, polygamous, teenage marriages were the norm, and they mainly lived off subsistence farming. Cultures were as diverse as the colours of the rainbow, rules and norms worshipped like the gods they so religiously believed in. There was a strong sense of community as well as politically structured empires led by kings whose thrones were hereditary. The land was vast, and as long as one adhered to the rules of the community, there was peace. They relied more on nature than we do now and from all I can gather, there were no Louis vuitton or Gucci despite the abundance of leather because clothes were largely meh; covering only the essentials of human reproduction. Life was fine, even great as far as I can tell. Trade business was thriving and kingdoms were growing even stronger and expanding rapidly. Sure, the chances of survival were diminished: if you survived the plague, you still had to battle neighbouring tribes looking to expand their territory, avoid being mauled by marauding wild animals, somehow become immune to witchcraft, pray and sacrifice regularly enough to the gods just so they don't inflict natural calamities. Nevertheless, I assume –by virtue of survival for the fittest– we would still have risen above all that. It might not have been a life of red carpets, the Kardashians or Netflix, but I'd honestly be game.

Many have tried to theorize what Africa would be like if the Europeans never came with any ill intentions of colonizing or imposing their ideologies. I understand that in those days, colonizing was the in thing where 'first come, first colonize' was the prevailing mantra and even the all mighty America was a victim but that doesn't justify anything. Africans from what I can tell are innately very warm people; it's only the greedy and ill-intentioned outliers that give us a bad rep. The teachings we get from a tender age resonate around values and respect for all and sundry; principles I find upheld to date. African mothers still whoop their children when they misbehave, that is coupled with eccentric literary expressions subconsciously passed down through generations of mothers and daughters. A culture that enunciates the value of respecting elders and visitors is inculcated the hard way and we all joke about it in versions of things African moms say and I see the same in the West where African Americans seem to have upheld the same in the name of "my momma" sayings. I don't know much about other continents and their perception of this gesture, but we take it very seriously and I assume that that was one of the reasons we were so welcoming of the Europeans.

I'd like to imagine the Brits before coming to Kenya were thinking of how big an opportunity travelling to a foreign land; fresh with resources and abundant with land was, especially during a time when an economic depression was occurring in Europe. I consider it to be kind of like the idea of inhabiting Mars if the technology just happens to be discovered and humans are free to inhabit, but this was even better as Mars was on earth; habitable and only a boat ride away. Am sure the missionaries and discovers talked about the existing people on a light mood, like, "Yeah, we found some guys up there mate, but it's all good, they have no idea, In fact, I think they can do some work for us for free." They have now shaped our continent quite literally. The scramble for Africa was so hot, they had to sit down somewhere and decide who would get what just so everyone would get a piece of the action. I guess 'twas the land grabbing season and we just happened to come in last, the most amicable I may add. The damage has been done, the continent has been divided, and the roots of African culture have been eroded and split by the European mantra of divide and conquer, and divided and conquer they did, like taking candy from a baby.

I attribute a huge percentage of the evils we Africans face now to the aftermath of colonialization, these same evils that are stacked up against us to christen us a shit-hole, underdeveloped or developing by standards we never even had a say in. We still bear the brute of Africans being shipped out to provide free labour just that the name has now changed from slavery to racism and in as much as African Americans might not fully identify with our sympathy for them; we still feel it in our bones. We hear stories in form of statistics of how African Americans ensure that American prisons are not closed by providing their able bodies as head-count to try and turn the tables on their minority status, even if it means doing so in confined spaces. They can go on trial for crime X or Y but we all know it a deep-seated boiling pot of frustration cum anger whose roots were grounded in the time of their ancestors. Essentially, they are put on the stand for evils they never had a say in. I can sit here and write all the but's to this proposition "...but everyone knows crime is wrong" "... but the law says" Yes, but don't forget that no one was born a criminal, it is the society that makes one. Ultimately, the same people who are discriminating against them with chants of "go back to where you came from" are the same people who brought them there, or at least their ancestors, and we've seen how de-linking these two is simply naivety we'd like to revel in to keep buried skeletons neatly tucked away in their graves rather than face a complicated truth. No one sets out to be discriminated; no one wants their odds of finding a job stacked up against them because of what happened before they were born. No one decides which family to be born in, otherwise I'd be son number one million, two hundred and sixty six point nine to the current leader of the free world, I know that, you know that, everyone knows that, but it all seems like a cock measuring contest for just the right combination of naivety and arrogance.

There was no consideration in terms of culture or language while setting the boundaries of the 54 countries whose names and capitals we try so hard to memorize; in essence, they are arguably boundaries of our love for one another, they are no more than just invisible lines that are the boundaries to progress. Let's look at the United States, roughly 300million people and less than 3 times the size of Africa but the state boundaries are more invisible, more so to the world of business. You don't need a visa to travel from state to state, launching a business in another state isn't a Mt. Everest climb, and yet for Africa, we have somehow confined ourselves to boundaries we never asked for in the first place. We are the best enemies to ourselves. If it wasn't for that scramble, it would have been the individual inhabiting communities that determined which region they occupied, trade would have been open to whoever was ready. We would have built governments the way we wanted. Gone through a normal growth trajectory that was defined by our own wars, economic crisis's, political atmosphere and what we believed in rather than going through the motions of an abrupt war that had us defending our land and to the imposition of a pre-dominantly capitalist society. We would have governments, but one's truly built by the people, for the people and based on the people's culture. We wouldn't have to worry about corruption because we would have developed a system around what we needed. We wouldn't have to grapple with constitutions written by foreigners in their own language supposedly crafted to our needs because we would have developed our own system by our own standards, and by our own people, thus avoiding any limitations of the language of law; a foreign one at that, or the whole constitution in general. Maybe it would have been a whole lot better than what we have now. Maybe we wouldn't be so discriminatory against women and minorities. Maybe we wouldn't live in fear because we don't all have law degrees and so we can't interpret the laws of the land let alone defend on infringed rights. Maybe, just maybe, if we were given the chance, we would have set a new development standard. So what if we never changed, who said development is a must!

If Africans were given room to embrace their culture, I don't see why we would have social evils associated with sex like adultery, fornication, rape or the famous daddy issues because foreign religions would have remained just that, foreign! And we would have remained with a polygamous society and teenage marriages that cancel out their whole premise. Sexual desires would be satisfied, boys would marry in their teenage years when they still have energy and a drive to fulfill the purpose of giving their families the best life they can provide rather than wanking away under their blankets every day of their teenage years earnestly awaiting their first sexual encounter at age thirty. They would make use of the so called 'good seed', a concept I have never quite gotten a grasp of, but still, if true, we'd have crosses of Angelina Jolie, Oprah, Nelson Mandela, Chris Hemsworth and Malala not Kim Jong Un, Idi Amin and all starving children. We would never have to play dating games; swiping on people's faces whether you like them or not. Marriage would be simple: girl meets boy and gets married. Not boy knocks over girl's books, gets her number, has a fling, dates till the fun runs out, dumps, knock over some more books and finds 'the one' only to divorce faster than you can say the word.

I'd never have to send memes to my classmates about how I'll murder the guy who invented formal education because they'd probably be no classes or education for that matter. At 22, I'd probably have 4 wives and 12 kids and a herd the size of my ego. My responsibilities would be limited, it would be the same routine over and over again: no bills to pay, no cheating allegations or videos and pictures online that are a threat to my alpha dominance. I'd call the shots in that house, if any of my children don't seem to respect that, I'll offer them as a sacrifice.

Ownership of property would just be one of those things, a community spirit is what I imagine would be encouraged rather than the capitalist society we have today.

I do not completely dismiss that by virtue of evolution and the curious nature of man that Africans would have made some kind of technological advancement similar to the West and the east, especially considering there would definitely have been exchange of culture in trade interactions. If the Europeans were a tad bit nicer, we would have exchanged ideas as well as set boundaries. We would have visited one another in good faith and helped build a global community that wouldn't be marred by hate, ridicule and the level of discrimination we have today. In a nutshell, all the bitterness and trauma wouldn't be there. We were denied the beauty of self discovery. The beauty of normal growth fueled by necessity rather than conformity. The beauty of falling down, faltering and fumbling to eventually dusting ourselves back up. Our learning curve would have taken a natural course aimed at 'winging it' as we go along from probable trial and error as opposed to pressure to grow too fast too quickly just to compete with standards we barely understood. It would have been our system; our baby; a virgin for us to deflower. As abstract as this may sound, one thing is certain: we were denied the thing we needed most: our childhood.

Sure, am speaking from a point that sounds full of resentment and it's very easy to misquote me, but the truth needs to said, Pandora's box has to be opened. We need to establish the stems of our problems by painting it black and blue to address them for closure and to understand the future a bit better. The white man set the bar a long time ago of what a good life entails: one run by a democratic government, has happy citizens, and one that's constantly trying to improve the quality of its people's lives and that's where the problem arises. In philosophy, the idea of what is moral and what is not has highly been debated, and in all the discussions I have had in my head, the conclusion has always been that we define our own sense of morals. You can walk around doing all that is required of you in your religion, but when your heart is not into it, then, when given the chance, you will practice what you truly believe in; and that's the radical kind of thinking I'd like to bring onto the table. No one person or state can say definitively that their mode of governance is the best or that the mark of success in a country is how developed they are or how happy the people are. It's always about the collective consensus of the people. They are the ones who determine their standards of success regardless of what others are doing. Having war machines is cool for a superpower country and eating dogs is cool in China but maybe it's not for us and doesn't have to be. The same way an individual's definition of success is defined by their unique childhood and genetic predispositions is the same way countries have unique definitions of success through their collective consensual ideologies.

We as Africans had our own definition of success before the Europeans robbed us of it. They imposed governance methods that our people weren't ready for. They imposed their way of life on us and we adopted it. Consequently, we have to work twice as hard because we are an 'inferior species', one riddled with lack of intelligence. No one plans to be born black or in a slum, or in poverty but it is about how we interpret our supposed short-falls. Nothing is wrong with you or your country until you say it is. I'd like to propagate a message to all Africans about how proud they should be for being African. So many of our people were killed for protecting and standing up for what belonged to them rightfully, I salute them all for giving us a voice.

What we have is magical; our history in itself is a tear-jerker, worthy of all the awards imaginable and most importantly, it's a story still in writing. Our grandchildren's children are reading every move we make and are waiting to take over from the crescendo we leave.

CHAPTER 3

Money.

◆ ◆ ◆

In the 1500's, Sir Johnson Harington invented a device we know all too well: the flushable toilet. It's where we read our magazines, catch up on memes, tweets and if you are like me, not using your phone on the toilet is just so 'unmillenial'.

The toilet ranks second in my list of 'not so impressive inventions'; right after money. Their commonality lies not only in their failure to impress me, but in their filth, though money trumps the crapper in this area; its filth surmounts cash; not in terms of germ-count or microbes, but in terms of the rot buried deep within. It is the formidable catalyst to the evil we see today. It's hard seeing a sad story on TV without somehow linking it to money. It's so powerful that it has the ability to shapeshift and disappears into our computers, and with no solid home, it's like a wandered, a sort of angel of death but one that still has the parallel ability to bring joy. Its beauty lies not in ink on paper or subsequent zeros after natural numbers, but in its power: insatiability; we have some, we need more, we have to have more, and it seems to never be enough. If prisons were to release all inmates whose incarceration is directly linked to money, all prisons combined would be smaller than the Vatican, and if all those whose charges had something directly or indirectly to do with money, I don't even know whether the term prison would be a thing anymore;

we'd probably rely solely on therapy and mental institutions.

I honestly think that the prisoners who have to sacrifice their freedom as a consequence of their wrong doings are sometimes better off. Out here, some are barely living; shackled by numbers on pieces of paper they once worshipped; It all sounds ridiculous when put in that perspective –I assume it's why, despite all those UFO 'sightings' aliens have never just dropped by to say a simple hello.

The issue of money is one we talk about in hush tones yet it forms the very circle around which our lives revolve. Talking about how much we earn is a taboo that existed long before I was born; in fact, we don't talk about the taboo of people talking about how much they earn because that's also taboo, and yet we think about it every day; It's our eternal subconscious to do list. Society has done an amazing job of painting a vivid picture of how worthless we are without money. We are made to fell undeserving of life if we don't have things; things that cost money and money we do not all have. We are bombarded daily with subliminal messages to spend, invest, donate, and buy things we don't really need just so we can feel more normal. They are everywhere and that's makes it so overwhelming. It's like being indebted to someone and seeing them everywhere but with just the right amount of self-control to not hold a gun to your head with a 'buy me' sign, but just enough to be condescendingly subtle. They encourage us to work harder so we can earn more and subsequently live more by having the financial freedom to buy the more and spend the more just so we can be more Homo sapiens sapiens than everyone else.

One instance where it dawned on me that I have very limited knowledge about money was when my dad stated categorically that I didn't. According to him, I did not understand the dangers associated with money. My mum on the other hand has always encouraged me to save, not in a flamboyant mother to son lecture, but as a footnote to a discussion where I was asking for money to do something only I would understand. I always considered myself the kind of person who saves without putting too much thought into it, but that was before I joined campus where things are different. It was a newer city that had ways to spend money on things that you could argue you needed: Ice-cream to cool off because it was hot, a new superstar in town who you just couldn't afford to lose a once in a lifetime opportunity to see, the new craze of ordering; quite frankly, overpriced pizza all at the literal touch of a button. There was just so much to experiment with that I just ended up going with the flow which I don't regret because I know am quite frugal in some other areas. Saving is great, having the self-control to maintain those saving is even greater, and breaking your piggy-bank after a successful saving spree is mind-blowing. I must admit that I am no expert when it comes to saving –sorry to disappoint you if that's what you were expecting. Am still learning the ropes but together, we can establish the fundamental ideas. I will share my lessons to try and delve further into this topic and provide deeper insight where you can derive your own lessons and hopefully learn a thing or two that you can apply in your own life.

Well, we are all here; our money-high planet so what now...? Do away with money? How would society function? ... What would be the new terms of exchange? I don't have the answer to that. Am not here to wave my millennial badge introducing a magical app that takes away all our problems or to talk about how 'crypto' is the next big thing. I don't plan on fighting money, even if I stood a chance, I don't think I have the muscle to fight it anyway; the strongest muscles in my body are in my fingers, and probably my stomach to type away bad things and to absorb all the caffeine typing those words. We have built such a strong social firewall around it that our purposes in life revolve around it; it's here to stay no questions asked. The best we can do now is play along with the game or so called rat race, and hope that the whale spits us out whole at the other end –hopefully the right end, if you know what I mean.

      Let's talk about the elephant in the room. Money vs. Happiness: an age old question that's been debated for centuries by the brightest and the not so bright. The idea of having more money makes us see how most of our problems can be solved by simply having it in abundance. It's true that lots of problems can be solved by simply throwing money at them and we don't even have to go that far to prove this, for example, am writing this book with the hope that it will get published, hopefully soon, and it really stresses me out thinking about all the nittie–gritties involved in the actual publishing of the book lest marketing it. Having money would take all this worry away. I'd walk into a publishing house with my bank statement in hand and they'd all bow chanting "Hail Martin... Oh great author!" Heck! I wouldn't even have to sell the book, I'd just hand out free copies since the main aim is to get people to read the book and propagate my ideas, and maybe even make a movie out of it. It's a bit of an exaggeration but in truth, money does equate to happiness: buying you mother a new house makes both you and her happy, getting the good grades you wanted even if you had to pay for them makes you happy, a new guitar, paying hospital bills for the less fortunate, taking a cruise for three months to the Bahamas sipping pina coladas, heck yeah! Where do I sign up? But it's only up to a certain point beyond which, your bank balance doesn't make a difference. A sudden incurable illness even in the best and most advanced clinics in the world might not really need your money, or for a plane soon to crash, the pilot might not really be of help even if you promised to bequeath your entire wealth in excess of a billion dollars to them. Ideally, a balance is needed in everything, take the instance of a shrink; it's common practice to only see a certain number of depressed patients beyond which it begins taking a toll. Knowing where to stop is quite essential not only to this practice, but also to other businesses, and the same applies to other avenues of life lest the initial effort becomes futile. A scrooge-like stock broker who denies himself of money pleasures with the ultimate picture of retiring at an early age of 35, may end up terminally ill just as he is about to achieve his target, and ends up regretting how he spent his life: saving and saving some more only to end up at the mercy of an illness that now reduces his efforts to blank stares at his wealth as nothing more than numbers on sheets of paper.

All our money making efforts are electrons revolving around the nucleus that is money. It is with no doubt that Plato said that all of mankind's efforts are geared towards seeking pleasure and reducing pain. When you think about it, it makes sense and I'd dare anyone to share with me an instance where an act -even an altruistic one- doesn't bring some form of pleasure to the doer. The popular statement, "I'd rather cry in a Range Rover than at the back of a 'matatu' (public transport van)," is one that has been argued by so many people and everyone seems to have their own opinion; whether it invokes religion or not. To further this bone of contention, the statement, intrinsically, is a derivative of the premise we looked at earlier on, which pre-supposes money's proportionality to happiness. The rationality of having a scenario where one is unhappy and rich seems improbable and completely ignored with unassailable naivety that draws on beggars riding horses rather than logic.

A widow somewhere in a slum is thinking of how hitting the lottery would help all her 9 kids get a proper education, better housing, and how she wouldn't have to wake up to a reality that's her life: the holes in the ceiling dripping with taunts that push her further into the hisses of enticing vices that are riddled with promises of a better world unworthy of the compromise.

Yes, there are so many problems that can be solved with money and we all glow at the idea of what we would do if our bank accounts grew times a hundred million. Am sure you've imagined sudden windfall that just hands you bucket loads of money at once? Some more often than others. Me? Well... not that much... just that my whole brain lights up like the playboy mansion from space when I do. I have index cards tucked away safely with notes; I could probably make a book out of it on demand. The first thing I'd do is withdraw enough notes to make a chair fort and then spend the next hour just throwing it all around, counting, throwing it around some more and then counting it again till am exhausted. I would hire my own team of avengers but with suits and better gender representation; they'd form my team of the most loyal and witty financial aids. Their first assignment: getting me the lowest risk investment returns.

All work with no play makes playing a whole lot more fun when you have money working for you. I would travel the world till an international cocktail of mould grows on my passport, buy crazy expensive art because that's what rich people on TV do, engage in bidding wars at auctions just to piss of billionaires because I can, buy caviar for my cat 'Schrödinger' and buy the rights to that name because it's cool and I can. It sounds so fun just thinking about it, and in essence, this is what we buy when we purchase a lottery ticket; the short-lived pump of dopamine fueled by endless thoughts of having the world at your feet, figuratively speaking of course. Don't be naïve though, there are dozens of stories out there of people who had the chance and blew it quite literally. It almost sounds like a curse. So, do these past instances mean that we should all embrace the proper trajectory of success and actually work our asses off to get there instead of simply fanaticizing about it? I'd have to kill you if I told you. I am just the right amount of naïve, I think about the downsides of a large windfall as well: I'd have to constantly look over my back thanks to my face being clownly paraded on every screen, my phone would light up incessantly; differently worded favours flowing in for the umpteenth time. It all sounds so stressful and that's not even half of it. It seems like the best thing to do is lay low and spend time growing up faster than you would have. The hidden joy of having money lies in people not knowing how much you have (no pun intended)–maybe that's why talking about how much we earn is a taboo. Now, when you strike sudden gold and your face is plastered all over the media holding that dummy cheque with an ear to ear ecstatic smile that has naïve written all over it, it's easy to forget that everyone else has fanaticized about holding that same cheque, and they all want you to do what they would have done with it, because everyone's way is the right way, so don't be rude, okay?

Our capitalist world has driven money to the peak of survival tools. It is those with plenty of it that are more equipped. It's at times daunting how much work one has to put in just to catch up. The most common issue that concerns the wealthy is trust, there are relatives out there who might treat them nicely but just as a facade in an attempt to get a spot on the bequeathment roll. It becomes so difficult when relatives are at your constant beck and call for favours because of your wealth and once the cycle starts, it never seems to break. That's one of the reasons families break up; the extended family lacks the shrewdness to contemplate a position of wealth and the accompanying responsibilities.

Money is a means to an end and not an end in itself and that's what makes it so useless at certain points in life. You pay for a movie to get the experience and to be happy, you buy a helicopter to ease movement and save on time; and we all know time is money. Just having money isn't what any one of us wants; it's the freedom that comes with it. The freedom to wake up and do whatever you want because the money allows you. Freedom to marry as many wives as you want because that's what some women are looking for, right?

To become rich and wealthy in the fastest and surest way possible probably has to be by starting a business, but it's not an idea we mostly entertain beyond banter because of the tedious amount of work involved. It's either that, or having been born with a silver spoon in your mouth. Business is the whole idea behind money and you really don't have to be that special to start and make profit. The whole idea around money is providing value to the human race: you play your sax for an audience or fix a broken pipe here and there and they pay for providing the service they can't themselves, that's the message we should all be spreading. The process should be appreciated and respected so shut up and stop whining about how society is unfair, stop dreaming about the lottery as your saving grace, just provide value and it will reciprocate. Apply the 10,000 hour rule and see what happens. Consistency is your best ally and I've found it to be rewarding in imaginable ways and situations like comedy. Read a book everyday for a year and see what happens, download a language app and practice 30minutes everyday and see what happens, save 100ksh a week for a year and see what happens, jog every morning for a year – especially if you are Kenyan– and we will both see what happens to you at the Boston marathon. Bottom-line, be invested in something so diligently and consistently and I guarantee that you will be rewarded; the heavens will open and bless you in ways you never knew one could be blessed, I dare you to prove me wrong.

I don't really know how much is too much when it comes to money because I've never been on the higher side of the spectrum, so I can't really speak for the 1%. Nevertheless, I've always felt like leaving billions just lying around in my account is not the legacy I'd like to leave. I've always envisaged making an impact on the world, and if I'm in a better position financially to do it, I don't see why not, you?

CHAPTER 4

The Internet.

◆ ◆ ◆

At age 12, I joined facebook. I was in class seven at the time; 2009 to be specific and had just heard about facebook on the last place people seem go to for news nowadays: mainstream television. I don't exactly remember what the context was, but it was the business segment and I remember thinking this would be the next site I would log on to the moment I got hold of an internet connection. The internet then wasn't such a big deal; at least not in Kenya; furthermore, a town known best for agriculture, but cyber cafes were a booming business in the town areas and the idea of a global network for me at the time, was just fascinating. My mum had just gotten a nokia 2630 and it was the only internet enabled phone in the house. Ironically, I knew how to use the internet on a phone but not a computer. This was how I registered and took my first profile picture in form of a selfie with the back camera –yes, yes, I know, I should have patented while I had the chance. It was and still is inarguably the best photo I've ever taken with a 5 megapixel camera with zero qualifications whatsoever in photography. I was wearing my favourite white-striped blue shirt at the time while standing in front of the beautiful green leaves of a plant we considered a flower and yet had no flowers, either way, it sufficed. I was stationed strategically, conscious of the lighting to capture the glowing shine on both me and the leaves. I remember thinking how amazing the picture was and the itch that followed to upload it. It was a stepping stone of history in the making; a stride in a direction that set the trajectory for the future of technology in my eyes. Going through my posts from said days makes me cringe and it never gets easier, or at least for me it hasn't; even with this book, am aware I might look at it at some point in the near future and wonder what the heck I was thinking writing that –I still do with every editing round but that's more a me problem so just keep reading.

I was curious and fascinated by the internet and social media as a whole ,I honestly think I did it all. My most cringe-worthy moment was lying to a girl twice my age –cat fishing is what they call it now. I was too young to have any ill intentions or be romantically involved so I guess it was just entertainment on my part; she could have been way older than I was, but I was cheekier. We'd exchange one message each day since, well, mum had to work and I had school, but that didn't make me any less occupied by thoughts of what we'd talk about next. I eagerly awaited mum to get home, take her phone, check the message, and then reply all in a day's work. Am not proud, I was naïve and stupid (weren't we all); I had no one to tell me what was expected of me and what was not.

Today, am not a fan of social media. I've always been proud of the fact that I started early: I joined instagram in 2013, did snapchat around the same time; sending those quick expiring photos to strangers abroad since it wasn't a thing here yet. What can I say, I was, and still am, a free spirit who was open to almost anything, it's a surprise I've never tried drugs. I went on to delete my instagram and snapchat but kept my facebook solely motivated by the need to maintain my contacts.

We are in a different space now. Connectivity and consequently social media has blown up and we are frantically running up and down to mitigate the negative effects that come with it.

The internet hasn't been here for long and truth is, it's a 'learn as you go' process. Unlike discoveries made long time ago that have undergone extensive research, we are still making baby steps when it comes to social media and the internet as a whole. To come up with proper strategies of approach, we need enough data to compile premises that will help us draw sober conclusions based on rationale. We are like guinea pigs for the future generation since there are still so many uncertainties on the effects of social media in the long term.

At one point, I felt so frustrated by social media and how I'd never heard anyone prescribe how to use it so I went online to search for answers. I couldn't find anything that met that need, it just added onto the pre-existing frustration of running blind. Everyone just seemed to sort of 'wing' it by doing what everyone else was doing –which essentially was also 'winging' it- and that to one who has been taught to rely on superior intellectuals for what to do, just yanks my brains out.

One of the vexing and yet laughable moments I have had on social media was this one time when I decided to give feedback on a TV ad from a very popular global brand that in my view was using sex appeal to advertise a product that had nothing to do with sex (don't roll your eyes at me, I was young). As the some-what idle and energetic youth I was, and brought up by a mother who comments on all 'badly dressed' women we see on TV, it was bound to rub off. So I messaged them and shared my two cents by expressing my opinion of how misleading the ad was through a personal message sent directly to their facebook page. "Who asked you?" was the response I got after they took their sweet and precious time. I was flabbergasted and quite honestly, hurt, it was like a stab, one that gave me an itchy brain trying to resolve what I had been taught by my parents and what this human being be-hind a keyboard was trying to teach me. I took my time to come up with a response. I knew I didn't want it to be in the heat of the moment, so I decided to be the better man and respond with a simple question that exuded rationalism and critical thought beyond my age. I wanted them to feel like jerks for being rude to me so I wrote back, "What happened to consumer feedback?" and am still waiting for their response to this date, maybe they are still busy holding a conference meeting since I'd thrown a 'hot one' their way –at least I thought so. This is what we see happening today on a personal level. In my view, the concept is not new, bullies have always been there, and will most probably always be there, it's just that they have acquired more power and a new fancier name: trolls. The wave of technology has made the world smaller and yet larger; consequently, we have pulled the bullies closer to us and in larger waves respectively. Psychologists tell us that bullies are just expressing their world by acting out, but that hasn't seemed to stop them. I personally abstain from social media not because I've ever been out rightly bullied or attacked, but because I don't want to create a facade that people can cling onto of how happy my life is when it's really a series of peaks and troughs because not everyone knows that. I must admit that at times, when am in a really good mood, I feel the need to let the world know, but it's honestly not from the point of "hey guys check it out, in your face!" but rather it's from a "am doing this because am normal and am genuinely happy about something I'd like to share with you" and in truth, no one really asked me, am a phone call or a text message away for those who really want to know. When it comes to social media, my perspective is one of providing value, scrolling pictures endlessly does not gratify me in any way other than making me feel pressured to double tap on people's pictures or like their posts just because they liked mine. I want to leave there having gained something other than weight from a depressive episode. I can't prescribe to anyone how to use social media or the internet as a whole, the best I can is to tell you to always remain on your toes; your greater well-being should and is always the bigger priority.

Teenagers are dying from depression because they can't live up to the expectation that the people they admire have set online. People on social media remind me of the perception I had long time ago about girls: I thought they were all angels who pooped gummy drops and peed fruit juice. I held them in such high esteem that the idea of courting was the preserve of a guy who oozed coolness; very hip clothing and heavy swagger to boot, and for them to go out with someone like me, you had to move heaven and earth just a fraction of a centimetre. I still hold them in esteem but I've busted the myths (I now know they don't just walk into bathrooms to gossip). I want to spark a conversation that breaks down social media for what it is. Acknowledging that we are only showing our good side in the posts we put up is the first step, the more we make that clear, the healthier it is to for people to open those apps. We need to take it easy on ourselves as young people, the images we all see on social media with all the glam and titles of social media gurus and influencers should not budge our self-esteem, if anything; they should boost it by inspiring us. We need to relax and understand that no one defines our happiness other than us. We are our own bosses and we define what it is we want and we make the universe give it to us. I have seen my fair share of vlogs, I've heard my fair share of all the 'hi guys' variations, vloggers hoping from one fancy store to the next, heading to trips we can only speculate the cost, buying things we know we can live without but suddenly need because we admire what we see and we want to be more like the people on the front-end of those cameras. Ultimately we end up craving that lifestyle; at least I know I have, and I know very well that for me to live up to those standards, I have to move money around and make lots of sacrifices here and there that are just not worth it to keep up with a 'Kardashian' lifestyle. We forget that for some of those people, it's just a hustle; they are paid to influence you to need the product they need your money for. So, don't take it too personally, just make clearer judgments from now on. I know it was fun when we never knew it was happening, now, I just feel stupid for knowing.

I don't need to drink 300kes worth of coffee or have Sauti

sol as my gang or Amina Abdi as my turn up girl. All I need to do is make what I have work right for me and not fret all the time about what's not right. There is something not right with all those people we think are at the epitome of success –yes, even Beyonce– and we forget that they are under pressure to portray a perfect image because it's the whole foundation of their hustle. You can walk down to a club and punch a bouncer at a club and it might not be news, in fact, chances are it won't make it onto social media, but not everyone has that luxury.

It hurts me that am not able to appropriately express emotions via text because the emojis for me really don't do justice; for one, I don't laugh that hard, I don't tear up that often unless the joke is really funny, and for crying out loud, am not yellow nor do I turn to green when am ill. I thrive better engaged in face to face conversations where we can both read the other 55% of our communication in the name of body language cues. I want you to see my true reaction and get my true thoughts real-time with the least latency possible. All these aspects of communication are completely ignored in phone calls and most of all, texting. Conversations online for me, and I suppose everyone, should ultimately lead to physical contact so we should try as much as we can to keep this end goal in mind.

It's interesting just imagining what the 22nd century will consider history. There is so much historical data to comb through; they will literally be viewing the world in our eyes. They will have audio and visual data that gives insight with a sort of time-lapse of how life progressed and how civilization itself has advanced. I dread being a master's student in that generation because I'd have to comb through more than twice the amount of material just to write a paper on a topic I've worked just as hard to find; the dynamics of evolution will hopefully give them something to write about so am not too worried about that.

One big downside to the internet and its concept of having

all the information you could ever think of at your fingertips is, you guessed it: too much information. This is one of my worst aspects about the internet. We have to scour through dozens of websites, dodge all those ads that you know are just malware in disguise just to find a sentence or two that contain what you were really looking for, –that is if you actually don't get bored– but this teaches us a valuable lesson; one that shows you that the internet is a tool and not the holy grail. Think of it as water in a lake but with unfiltered garbage floating on top, garbage we have to sift through to get to the final bottle-worthy product. Once I pop open Google and type in what I want, I see a ton of sites that are all clamouring for my attention. When I think critically about it, some of these are just bloggers who really aren't experts in said field but are looking for traffic. It's like a public library, but one where anyone can write just write a book and immediately shove it into one of the shelves. It's like an online version of survival for the fittest (may the best SEO win). You'd think those that ask you to pay for the information are the gurus in the field, but it's sadly not always the case and at times, you have to learn this the hard way.

There is also some sort of pressure on young people brought on by this fingertip information. They now need not only to learn the oxford dictionary, but also the urban dictionary just so they can fit in everywhere and still standout. Today, I had said that I'd try to learn more about the stock market and just the other week I did the same with North Korea and I now know more about both than the average person does. There's pressure not just to learn everything, but everything and more. The construct of our governments require that we all become lawyers otherwise we don't know when our rights are infringed on or what to do when they are. We've figured that the only way we can stop simply ranting on twitter and clinging onto hashtags to express our grievances to our leaders is by using the same law to threaten them when they don't admit accountability and that requires knowledge from being well read.

CHAPTER 5

Men vs Women.

◆ ◆ ◆

I average about one match on Tinder every two months and that's after swiping every day, out of which, I only initiate conversation with one in every three matches simply because my swipes are determined more by mood rather than sober judgment –I once swiped right on a girl called 'Mojo' just so I could craft creative banters around the antagonist in powerpuff girls if we matched. For those unaware, tinder is a dating site that allows you to find a match by swiping on their photos; you swipe right if you like them and left if you pass. My radius of finding potential suitors is set to the maximum, I have a full bio with more details than a professor's resume and a prevailing bare minimum of four photos all meticulously curated through a fire-cast process that overcritically overanalyzes ever tilt, shadow and aperture of the eye. This is the reality of dating for 'millennials' today, well, maybe not this exact scenario, but the wave of the internet disrupting our social structure to the extent that our values and morals can't seem to keep up.

Tinder is only one example of the dynamics in the dating scene; it's a millennial mindset that gives the term obsolescence a run for its money. Emphasis is on getting there faster rather than embracing the long-standing due diligence process. Consequently, relationships seem to be competing against one another;

clothes are thrown off faster than they are put on and marriages end faster than we can say the word divorce. Am not one to give relationship advice since I've never really been in a serious one and the only experience I really have claim to is from observing, reading, watching other people and deriving lessons from their experiences. Clearly, from my tinder example and my lack of first-hand experience, am not worthy to sit at the throne of relationship gurus and neither am I one to ask let alone give advice, that, I leave to the likes of Steve Harvey, I've watched a lot of his clips and he tends to give solid advice to women; I've learnt a thing or two about what women really want, he adds a comedic ring to it that makes it a whole lot more interesting to watch as well as listen. He sometimes brings on men and women to try and play match maker and the most fascinating thing for me is when the one searching for love is asked for what they are looking for in a man and they state the obvious, something cliché like, "I want a man who is loving, caring and appreciates me," yeah right! Cause all the other women are looking for men who could not care less and who don't appreciate anything about them. It's interesting and leads me to question whether we can really summarize what we are looking for in our spouses or whether even given the opportunity to make an infinite list with all the qualities we want, that would be of any effect in increasing the percentage of our compatibility with our match.

Society has given us the basic guidelines of attracting almost any woman or man: For men, the physical trademark seems to be tall, dark, and handsome; being buff gives you a serious edge. For the personality aspect, women want a man who is a gentleman and who is compassionate, honest and all those good qualities in that line. In terms of spiritual, most African women want a man who has deep faith in God or the associate religion. For mental, they want someone who is driven, one who has goals that seem achievable, one who oozes drive and actually does something about it. One who is able to support them and keep them emotionally in line when they have their moments. One who doesn't show emotion and yet shows emotion. One who will love forever and stay by their side even when they throw tantrums that are more of a catharsis than a cry for help. One who is able to stand down when the wife is right because we all know they are always right. One who kisses them in the morning and sends texts in the middle of the day confessing love, and one who sends flowers to the office for everyone else to gawk at and feel a tad bit awful about their own unsatisfactory lives. One who isn't too busy but is busy enough to always have something going on and to provide for the family. One who hasn't been with too many women or any for that matter but still knows how to hit it right. One who has never experienced their first kiss just so they could experience it together for the first time and yet, be an expert at it with all the right motions, techniques that even Romeo can't match. A real man with a voice for days that makes everything sound better in deep assurance, one that makes her melt every time they talk on the phone with vibrations that make her feel like a tremor force in her body vowing to take over. Wowee! This is not that kind of a novel, let's not get carried away. That's the basic gist of what I think women want, they have broadcasted it so many times to us that it's at the back of our minds –I assume some men just choose to ignore.

For men, the basic framework of what we are looking for in a lady seems to be one who is beautiful, motherly, and has an accentuated body shape with all the bells and whistles in the right places. For the emotional, she needs to be a whole lot more emotional than the guy; she needs to cry when in a situation that should warrant crying. She needs to be needy emotionally but just enough that she provides that emotional push to the guy when demanded. For mental, she doesn't need to be too preservative about putting out, she should put out but not too much to be rendered slutty. She should play hard to get but not too hard that she can't be gotten. She should be a virgin but somehow magically good in bed. She should be vulnerable but not a wimp. She should be independent but not overpowering. She should let the man be the head of the house. She should be a girly girl that likes red lipstick and flowery dresses. She should make other men jealous not only of her physical beauty but also her intellectual prowess, but should draw the line when it comes to flirting. She should be more fertile than the Promised Land sprinkled with every animal's urine.

It's great that we understand each other to this level but I feel like we have set a new standard that's a somewhat rebel to marriage. Men and women now seem to be afraid of being tied down, everyone wants all the good things that marriage has to offer but no one seems to be willing to handle the negative repercussions associated. Divorce to me doesn't seem like an intrinsically evil thing; I see it as a way out that forces our reclaim of happiness, maybe it's just the vows and the general current marriage framework that's flawed for 2019, but we can't outrightly dismiss it as an option. We tell our friends who are in bad jobs not to compromise on their happiness, and am sure it's a philosophy you my reader believe in. You can't remain unhappy just because you don't want to taint the statistics. I've said that depression is a normal reaction to a radical negative change that needs just as radical ideas to overcome with immediate urgency and divorce is not that different, it is about claiming your happiness even if an unhappy divorce is the ultimate decision; I however still acknowledge that it is a difficult process that involves more dynamics than what I've put on paper. I think the better emphasis should be put on the process of courting, we need to understand that these standards are as a result of unrealistic expectations created by the media and only exist in that same media; the idea of a perfect man and women is feasible but only on paper –or on screen. It is our upbringing that shapes how we behave in society and drawing from that, there is no such thing as the perfect spouse since we are who we are because of the myriad of factors that determine our psychology all the way from conception, and subsequently have little or no control over, the results of these are us behaving according to the subconscious framework created by these factors. With this, expecting the perfect spouse is impossible and we all need to give up on that idea by separating fiction and reality. Two, we need to give up on the idea of "the one" but I think this is an issue many have already made peace with, but definitely worth not overlooking. I can't tell you what percentage you should be looking for, but one thing I have come to terms with is the fact that to find a higher percentage match, you have to meet and talk to a lot of people just so you can refine your taste with what's actually available.

I've always held the opinion that women don't know how men really think; the same way they claim we men don't understand how they think. Men are highly motivated and their brains are constantly racking for the next big idea or project they will be working on. They don't as enthusiastically entertain the idea of mundane activities that are circular in nature like washing dishes as women do, and the biggest way to prove that is with the nature of conversations on both ends. For women, discussing social issues and talking about other people seems to come naturally to them and I perceive that as an inclination brought in by their nature as a caregiver and the emotional stronghold of any house. Men are generally more inclined to talk about grand ideas that are inclined towards taking care of their family's security whether financial or physical protection. They are however still wired in a way that doesn't leave them completely self-reliant; they require reassurance at times when the going is tough, they need to feel stable emotionally and that's where women come in, they provide an anchor, a sense of consistency that keeps the men going and empowered. Women love the small things, they thrive in consistency, a thing I think us men take for granted, women love things like cleaning, doing things like makeup for a whole hour in the morning just for the day with all the intricacies of applying a little bit here and a little bit there meticulously which to me sounds frustrating just talking about. They like the nittie gritties that drive us men mad. They are more emotional and we all know and understand the value of that, their subjectivity drives most of their actions and for women who want to ooze power, they have to put that aside and that's why they are passed off as tough, arrogant, and more masculine than feminine because it doesn't conform to the gender norm we are used to. This same subjectivity is what makes them difficult to understand because of the nature of the annexed unpredictability.

Gender equality is a facade, one that has metamorphosized from the intrinsic desire of women simply wanting a bigger say. In reality, men being equal to women is unrealistic, something we will never achieve. The whole idea of why we are constructed differently is the primary difference we should be focusing on. We have just discussed some aspects that make us so different from one another and it's clear that we complement each other in more ways than one. Women can give birth and men cannot (Arnold Schwarzenegger aside) it comes with maternal instincts that us men do not have. Men are generally more willing to take risks and therefore bring forth the majority of radical ideas that change the world every day. Women are not as sturdy as men and therefore, some jobs are just not physically suited for them. Our perception of sexuality is very different, when considering sex, the way of thinking is not the same; the levels of testosterone that determine sex drive in both men and women are in different worlds. Self-love in the context of men is normal that some even admit to never being taught but for women it's different, thus a conversation that I find as a futile attempt debating with those who lack the understanding or whose biology creates for them a bubble outside of which is negative deviant behaviour.

We all find pride and joy in coexisting especially because of our differences. We don't want any sex to feel belittled. What am trying to do here is to extrapolate the strengths of each gender that make them unique or give them an advantage over the other gender. We complement each other and that's what we should be embracing. We can't have a level playing field because the game was already rigged before we came in to play, even education with all its holistic attempts to encompass everyone falls short of giving a fair opportunity of learning, when adolescence hits, that's when the differences become defined and we should stop trying to quash said differences but try to understand and embrace them. The greater struggle should be with issues that are fundamentally grievous involving the men and women whose acts and words express hate. I love and appreciate women because of what makes them women, they have qualities I do not find in men and that for me is an asset we seem to be hanging on a cross rather than tapping for its last drop of honey. I don't want to be equal to them because it's about complementing each other. The spotlight should not be on giving everyone the same opportunity, is should be making everyone the best version of themselves. We should stop trying to change what shouldn't be changed; the beauty of being a man or a woman, that for me is the true definition of gender equality.

CHAPTER 6

The Perfect World.

◆ ◆ ◆

I remember watching the movie, 'the god's must be crazy' a while back and there was this powerful statement that gripped me, it highlighted how in the wild, animals have learnt to adapt to nature, and in the city, where all of civilization lives, humans have made the world adapt to their nature in the name of building infrastructure and systems that make life a lot more convenient even if it means disrupting nature's eco-system. The movie had a scene contrast of small blades of grass seemingly week, brown and timidly swaying to the city's rhythm somewhere on the kerb of a highway clearly mocking the city and yet standing tall to prove its existence and as a re-affirmatory representation of mother-nature's formidable power.

I have always had the crazy idea in my head that the best life I can ever achieve would involve moving to an island somewhere completely cut off from civilization, not because am not smart or strong enough to conquer the world as it is, but because the life I envisage there is one free of any form of oppression, prejudice, hate, theft, crime, stress and anything about today's world that makes it seem like an awful place. Yes, I would be running away from problems but wouldn't you if given the chance? I yearn for a permanent vacation where all I have to think about is fulfilling the basic instincts of mankind. I must admit that life there would not be interesting as it is today going by the current standards, but there's a thick border between happiness and amusement.

We talk about how awful social problems are all the time. Whether it's triggered by that heartfelt documentary that aired on the 9 o'clock news last night that gives us something to rant about, or some juicy story about a celebrity who did something odd or did someone else other than their spouse, we all have our opinions and it's micro-stories like this that drive conversations on the social issues at hand and push everyone to highlight their opinion on what went wrong where and possible solutions regardless of whether it's just mere chitter-chatter. Sometimes, it really takes off and the conversations become a cause that gets things done; lawyers are involved, demonstrations organized, t-shirts printed and hash tags tweeted and that's a good thing but to what ultimate effect? I understand that every society has problems; it's a cycle that seems to be in an endless loop that one could even conclude that the term society is derived from societal problems. It's a cycle that also keeps us rather entertained to say the least and one that psychologists from all over the world have dozens of explanations for depending on the school of thought drawn. These problems are social because they have been constructed by us; their existence is piggy-backed on our very existence. Am sure at some point you have remarked "the world sucks" and it's true, it does suck; we have so many issues and we don't seem to really be making any headway, and when a solution is applied, another problem metamorphosizes and the cycle continues. We have to go back to the drawing board and ask what we really aim to achieve with all these holes we are trying to fill with patches. At what point will we humans look back and simply be happy in perfection? Some say perfection lies in imperfection, does it? Is there really a perfect world we are aiming at and what does it look like? What's the bigger picture we want? Is it better roads? Better healthcare? Higher minimum wage? Is this what truly makes us happy? Is all we want in Kenya or the world at large no more corruption? If we get all those, what next? And after those, what next?

I've been trying to crack the code and am happy to reveal that I now have it: the 'perfect' world. It's been stewing in my brain for years now so take a sit and enjoy the broth. Disclaimer: if you are a believer in perfection lying in imperfection, am sorry, that goes out the window. I hypothesize about what a world of pure happiness looks like? One where all social problems are eliminated: no divorce, no drug abuse, no capitalism, no suicide, no money problems, no financial crises, no fetishes, even bad weather here is a non-issue, a general world that knows no man-made evils.

Firstly, this life has to be built on a foundation; we have to identify and tackle the pre-existing problematic fundamentals so we can invert them and develop a concrete base for our world. My world is based on three principles: simplicity, full dependence on nature and ignorance; all principles constructed to go straight for the roots of this world's man-made problems. The idea of simplicity is built around the problematic fundamental that us humans are involved in too much shit we don't need and that exist to our amusement and masked detriment. This shit that leaves us always on our toes, waiting for the tipping force to push us into the abyss. From the moment you wake up, you have to think about your kids –if you have any–, make sure they are clean and bathed on time for the bus, make sure the waiver form for that school trip is signed, check emails to see whether Becky from HR replied, remain conscious of the water bill, rent, electricity bill, internet... there is just so much to handle, especially in the city, you never really get breaks when you need them because life is moving too fast. Forget the traditional biological clock, now, we have one that does not in any way discriminate on gender. There is the fear of missing out or 'FOMO' as we know it. There is an unvocalized pressure to travel, drink, go on expensive adventures that can only be done when we are young and in reality, the money is never enough so ultimately what you end up with is youth who are overworking themselves, stretching their budgets, and burning through money in chase of youth. There are little or no savings, and after the youth phase is out and family is in, there is the realization that there isn't enough room. It's these small things that in the end cause so much stress to the mind of a young person but to a lesser extent everyone who considers themselves modern or hip. So let's eliminate all that and make life as simple as we can; reduce our needs to the most trivial and compulsory and see what we get.

The second principle of full dependence on nature is inspired by animals, and the biggest inspiration is my cat Schrödinger; it's the holy grail of this whole discussion as my world is an envy of these creatures. As I write this, she's somewhere out there playing with grass or chasing moths while am here trying to win a Pulitzer. She lives like a queen –no pun intended. In her whole lifetime here on earth, she has never opened the door yet every time there's is a scratch or so much as a faint shrill, someone's there to open it. The tinniest of meows are enough to make me aware of her presence, she commands power because she never abuses it, her meows pierce the air in proprietary fashion, an indication that she is in need of something or you just stepped on her tail by accident. Ignoring her calls for more that 5 minutes makes you feel awful about yourself, like a heartless douche-bag with no empathy. Her face is undeniably too cute to ignore and the innocence they all posses makes them have a personality we all wish to harness and implant in people. I have never seen her with a handbag justifying it with the need to carry a bone that she thought might need a good gnaw later on if it so happens there's no catch, because nature is sufficient enough to provide food. There's no tissue needed to get rid of those messy moments because nature again, has provided one that's attached to the body and even better because it is versatile. She has never said a word I could comprehend, all I hear are those monotone meows and occasional purrs, and yet, we live in perfect harmony. She has no curfew, she goes and comes as she pleases to and from only God knows where. I could go on and on but bottom line is, nature is sufficient in its raw state to sustain life, all we have to do is to have absolute faith in it just like animals do.

The third principle is ignorance. Yes, we are the smartest beings on earth, or so we think. I've always entertained possibly the most ad hoc of thoughts: the idea that us humans being more rational than animals is nothing more than an ego massage. I could argue that they can philosophize, and maybe they just came to the conclusion that the unexamined life is just not worth examining –I certainly could– and they have us human beings to provide a whole pool of premises to forward that argument. So maybe Socrates was wrong; maybe the examining life is a recipe for disaster and is therefore not worth the trouble. We view the lives of animals as boring, they never get to experience the joys of surfing the internet or watching that funny 'meme' thats been the talk of the town. They have never experienced the joy of playing video games or travelling the world like we do. We can fairly agree that all these are assumptions; we haven't really had a proper conversation with them to ascertain that our lives are more advanced and consequently happier, maybe; just maybe, they could actually be smarter than us. Maybe sometime in the past they created a world that's kind of like ours and discovered that the ideal life is one of ignorance. Maybe they look at us today and see the misery in our eyes. Maybe the idea of rationalism could actually be a curse. We try to read more, to please more, to make more money, but why? Just to be happy? Who said that's where happiness lies? Are more cars what make us really happy? Is our standard of happiness the same as that of animals? Let's not forget that happiness is nothing more than chemicals that cause a sense of euphoria. I can provide you with dozens of stories that prove that the life of a stupid person is happier than that of an in-tellectual. An ignorant man worries less about making more money and thrives in the contentment of what they have, they appreciate the things life has blessed them with, they revel in the immediate happiness that's around them rather than the chase of said happiness, they are the ordinary people that work hard and pause to enjoy the fruits of their labour. A curious mind seems to be our poison, it leads us to wonder what's beyond what we can see and from a rational perspective, it seems unnecessary, despite our itch to explain everything, we really don't need to see what's beyond the horizon. When we take on too much, it takes a toll on us so why not just be ignorant and ignore the world as it is, admit that a rational life fueled by satisfying curiosity is good, but a life where we don't care is better. Ignoring all other factors, imagine not having a car versus having one. Having a car takes you in circles quite literally, it adds onto your responsibilities and we have already established that we need less of those not more: you have to think about fuel money, insurance, when the next service is due just so you don't miss it, and God forbid something happens and your car is involved in an accident. You live in a world of fear and paranoia about what might happen next while on the road. Maybe someone will swerve and cut in while in traffic and your road rage will go on a purge spree. There's a loan on the car so you have to be careful while keeping your other aspects of life in check or else the auctioneers come knocking and the house you toiled for years to save up for goes up on the market just like that. All this and so much more can be avoided if you were ignorant not just about the car, but also all the other unnecessaries of life. What if you embraced the trivials of life instead and reduced all the anxiety warranting tit-bits to rubble; reveling in the idea that by being ignorant you are quite indeed being smart.

We've established the fundamentals of our world so let's go ahead and build it.

It's a life that resembles the story of Adam and Eve in the bible; just a quick recap, these were the 'first beings' on earth, Adam came first and then when he got bored, he told God that he needed company that was one more his kind. So God sent Eve, the woman who was Adam's apple to his eye. Life there was great in my view, it was a jungle, green all over, –like the Amazon I assume. Creeping, crawling, and walking animals all of whom never harmed man because he had authority over them. They never read books, filed taxes, went to court, therapy or to the supermarket because nature was sufficient. All they had to do was name the animals and not eat fruit from one tree –spoiler, they did– but that's not what we are here for. I want you to imagine this life; it was so simple that I feel guilty using complicated words to describe it. It was simply that, life. Waking up to pointing some animals and blurting out a word, eating fruits and veggies straight from the soil and spending all the time in the world quite literally –because they lived like a thousand years which is no wonder since their whole diet was a cleanse and all they pooped, I imagine were seeds– and finally spending your life with the love of your life in the jungle naked, what more could a guy ask for.

I want us to imagine this kind of world but without all the biblical innuendo. Imagine waking up in the woods; you slept at the last place you felt like lying down because beds aren't a thing. You never needed a duvet, or a comforter or a mattress or a bed because the world is your bedroom, your territory, your room and your hair is your blanket. You don't know the time because you wake up when you want: when a need presses you either to procreate, eat, excrete, or protect. You don't have to get to work because your primordial needs are all the work you will ever have. Next to you lays no one because you don't have to marry, as a man; your work is done once it is done if you know what I mean. As a woman, you nurture your child till they are teenagers and then you show them the door, or in this case, their instincts just cause them to wake up and leave when it's time. They don't need you, they also don't need school because all the knowledge they need is either intrinsic from birth or derived from you the parent. All you need is to feed and protect; forget diapers, onesies and baby walkers. Showers aren't mandatory and clothes aren't even on your mind. You wake up and go where your instincts lead you. Every man has his territory. It's not overcrowded because nature has a system that somehow keeps everything in check. The mortality rate ensures that only those who are able to depend on the environment survive. Consequently, no one fears death like we do now because there is no obsession with what happens when people die, there is no religion to tell us what to do and what not to do, more so because people are moral without even trying. Reproduction is not complicated, it's still pleasurable, but its purpose is the core driver; there are no beads, plugs or toys to play around with because sex is fun but not for fun. There is no infidelity because no one owns anyone. There is no body shaming, anorexia, fat people, skinny people or self-image issues because no one cares about appearance and everyone is basically equal. Travel is only for survival so no cliché "I want to travel when I get money" remarks. You don't need doctors of medicine because you are too busy living and enjoying life to be a hypochondriac or to worry too much about the future. In your lifetime, you never have to utter a word because the world is too simple, everything revolves around the 4 basic instincts so a simple growl or grunt to express emotion will do. Mental disorders are not a thing because there are no triggers, there is subsequently no suicide because there is nothing to be depressed about; death is a normal process and is treated as such. There are no phones, or the internet, when you need to talk to a friend, you just head on over to their territory. You don't need the birds and bees talk because birds are just flying animals and bees are just flying nectar suckers. Killing is only when necessary and for survival, not pleasure so no psychopaths. No one would have to deal with bigot, misogynistic, racist, corrupt, nepotistic, fund-embezzling leaders because nature has provided order. No addictions because life is too simple to be thinking about that stuff. Finally, God is not a point of discussion.

ACKNOWLEDGEMENT

I'd like to thank the people who supported me in this daunting task. I found great encouragement in your moral support.

Please check out more of my content on my blog : martinchomba.co.ke